SOLOS

for the

HARP

PLAYER

Selected and Edited by

LUCILE LAWRENCE

ED. 2628

G. SCHIRMER, Inc.

DISTRIBUTED BY
HAL•LEONARD®
CORPORATION
7777 W. BLUEMOUND RD. P.O. BOX 13819 MILWAUKEE, WI 53213

CONTENTS

Preface

Among the *Solos for the Harp Player* are some transcriptions never before published as well as reprints of earlier editions by Carlos Salzedo. Of these transcriptions Henri Expert, the French musicologist, said he considered Salzedo's use of embellishments to be eminently suited to the Classical Period.

The Cabezon *Pavanne a l'italiana* and his *Four Part Fugue* were written for plucked string instruments of the 16th century. The modal qualities of these works have been kept rather than indicating optional accidentals which would make them conform to later tonal developments. The late Edgard Varèse brought these lovely pieces to my attention and I am grateful to him.

Dewey Owens has made some excellent selections of classical works which will give the performer and teacher some badly needed material that can be played well by the intermediate student.

The modern works in this album illustrate the point made in *ABC of Harp Playing* — that composers who do not play the harp can produce thoroughly playable and effective material for the harp, providing they collaborate with harpists.

Looking Glass River by Rudolf Forst was suggested by the lovely poem of Robert Louis Stevenson. Wen-chung Chou's *Chinese Folk Songs* are not specific folk songs, rather, they are traditional melodies of the kind used to accompany poetry. Alois Srebotnjak's *Preludes* have been performed in Holland at the Van Beinam Foundation's Harp Week Seminar and in Israel at the International Harp Contest.

L. L.

Index by Composers

Note

0   Harmonics are written where they actually sound; they are made on the string an octave lower.

   Eolian Flux.

Brassy Sounds: produced by playing with the fingernails very close to the sounding-board.

To muffle.

   To muffle with the left hand, a chord (or a single note) played with the right hand, or vice versa.

To muffle a specified group of strings.

Individual mufflings.

To muffle totally.

To isolate a sound from a preceding sound.

L.V.   To let vibrate.

A dot above or under the fingering or at the end of the placing sign ( ) means to leave after a note, that is, not to connect.

   Eolian Chords. Slide as rapidly as possible across a group of strings: upward (arrow pointed up) with the 2nd, 3rd, and 4th fingers, according to the fingering indicated; downward (arrow pointed down) with the thumb.

To slide with suppleness along a string, from the center to the top and vice versa. This sliding should be effected on the note which is written after the sign.

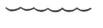   Guitaric Sounds: produced by playing very close to the sounding-board.

   Tympanic Sounds: Strike the most sonorous part of the sounding-board with the tip of the 3rd finger.

1

Pavane

Transcribed for Harp by
Carlos Salzedo
(1927 - revised in 1958)

Unknown composer
XVI century

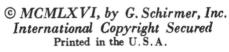

Italian Pavane

Transcribed for Harp
by Lucile Lawrence

Antonio de Cabezón
(1510 - 1566)

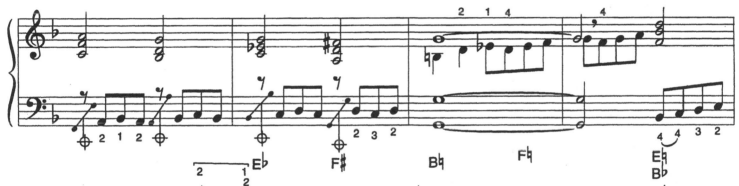

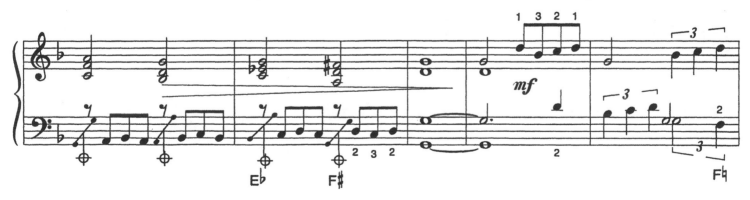

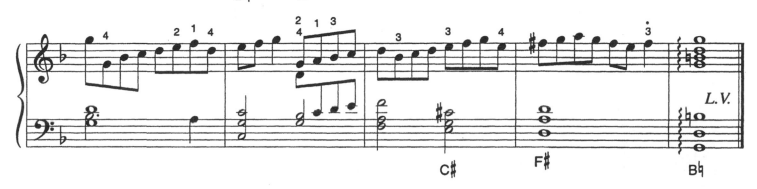

Fuga

Transcribed for Harp
by Lucile Lawrence

Antonio de Cabézon

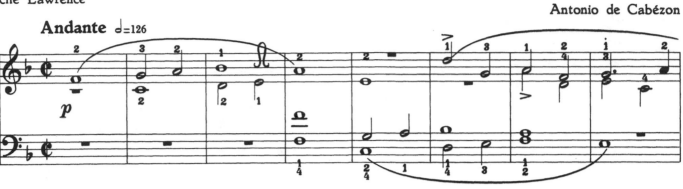

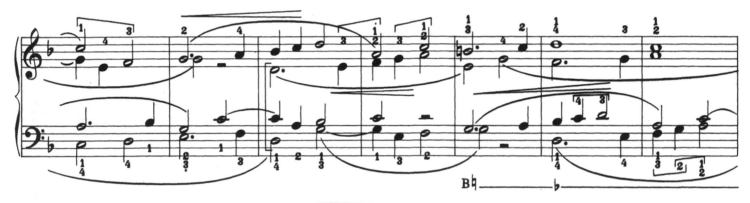

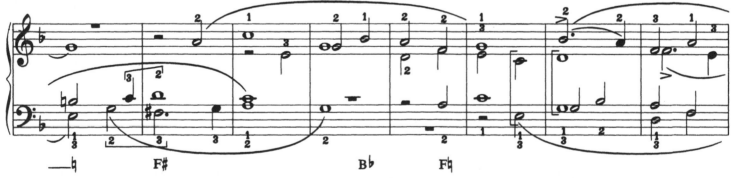

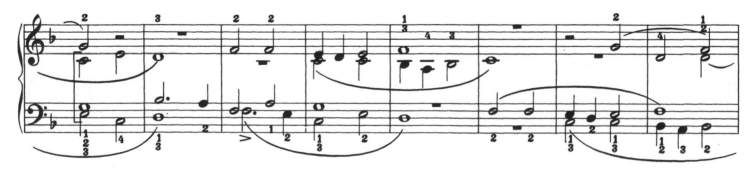

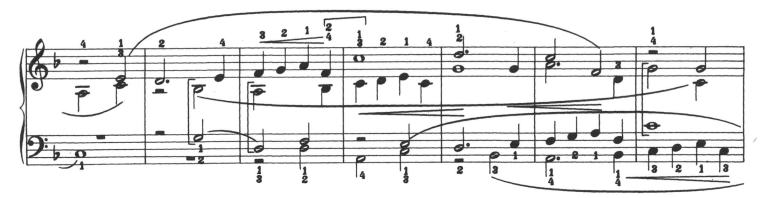

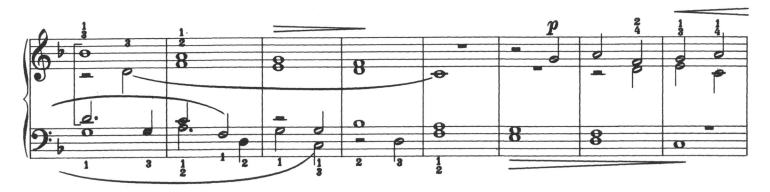

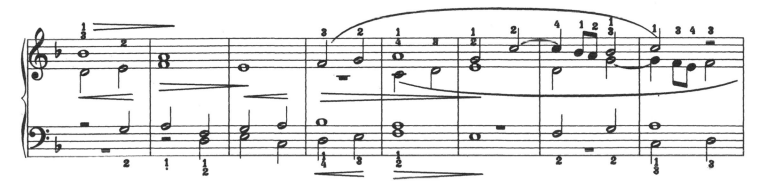

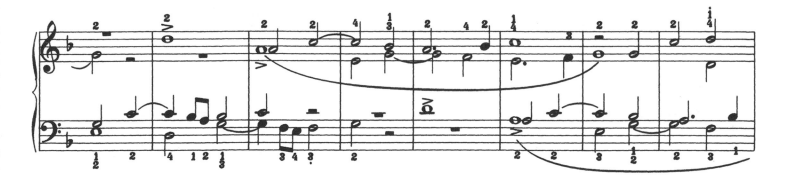

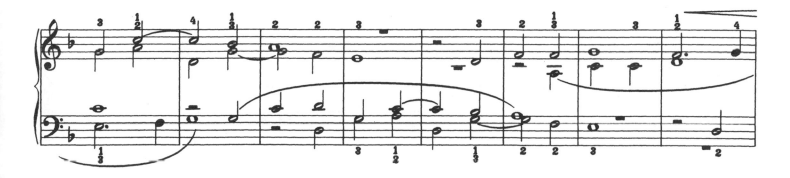

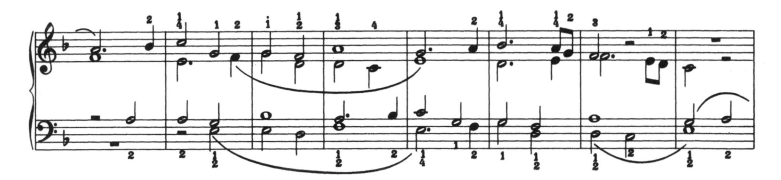

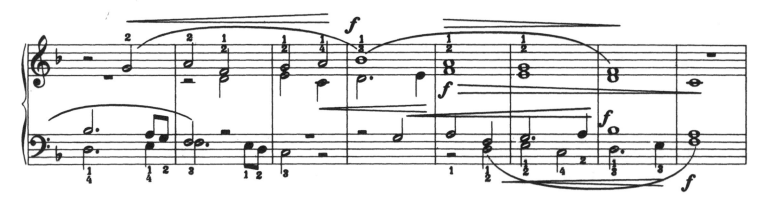

Giga

Transcribed for Harp
by Carlos Salzedo

Arcangelo Corelli
(1653 - 1713)

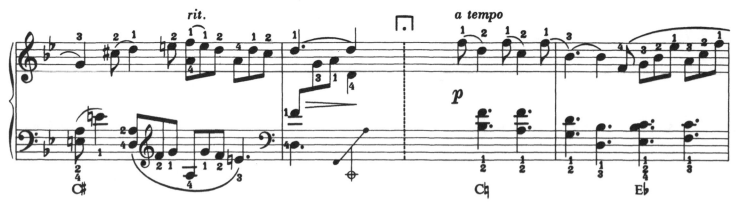

(1) In this piece, harmonics are written where they actually sound; they are made on the string an octave lower.

Sarabande

from Sonata VII, Op. 5

Transcribed for Harp
by Dewey Owens

Arcangelo Corelli

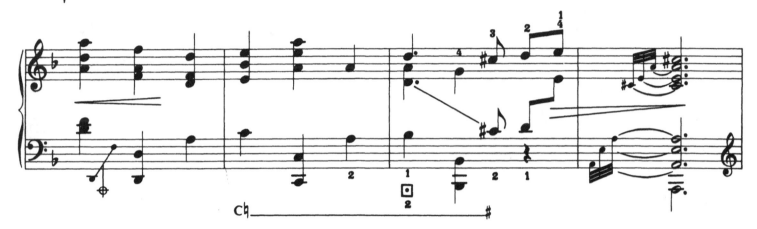

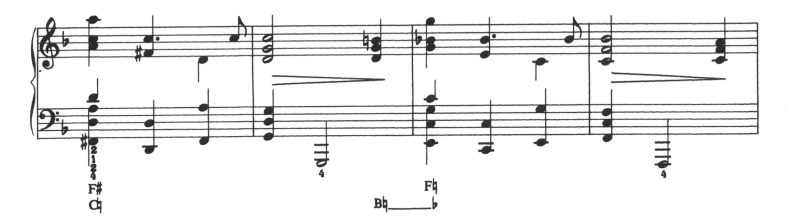

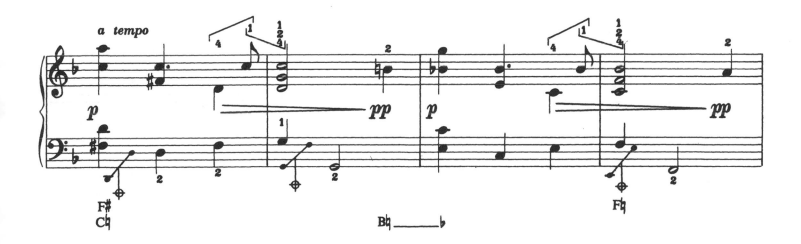

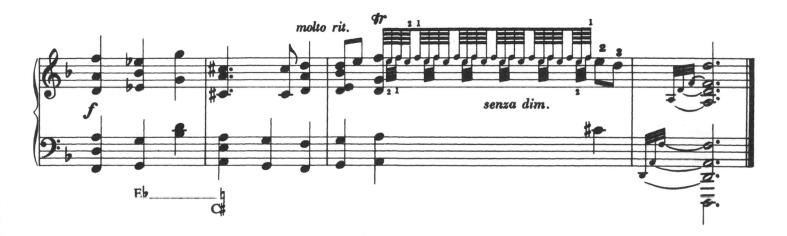

Gavotte

Transcribed for Harp
by Dewey Owens

Arcangelo Corelli

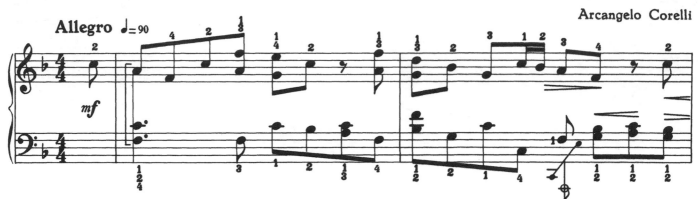

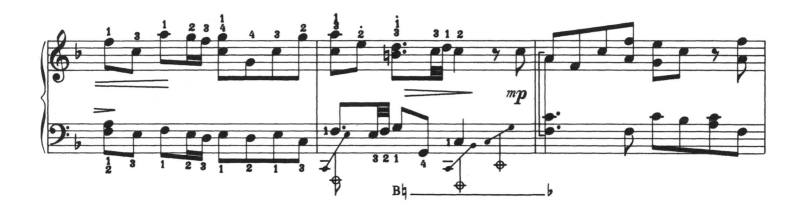

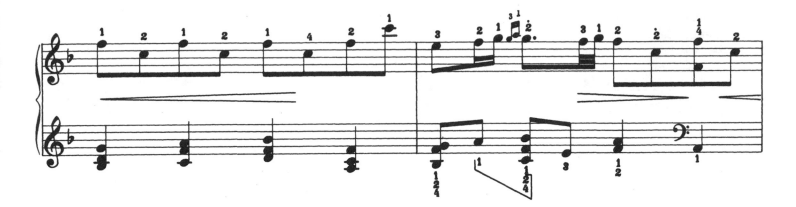

Rigaudon

Transcribed for Harp
by Carlos Salzedo
(Revised 1952)

Jean-Philippe Rameau
(1683 ~ 1764)

PREMIER RIGAUDON

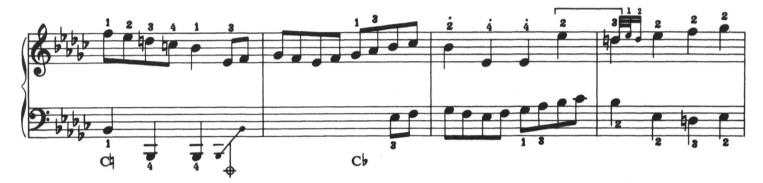

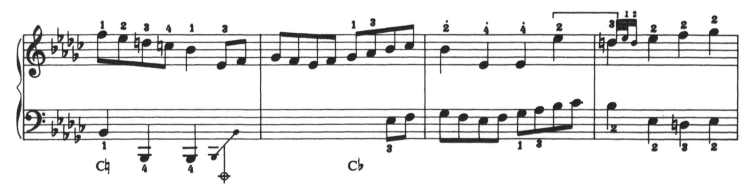

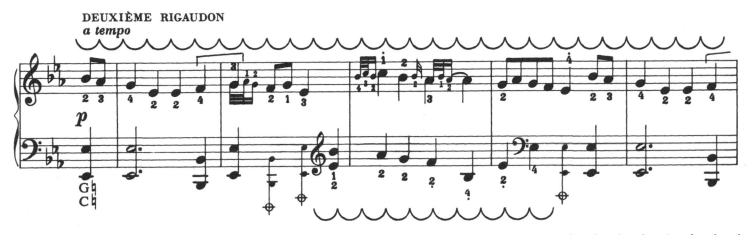

DEUXIÈME RIGAUDON

20

DOUBLE DU DEUXIÈME RIGAUDON

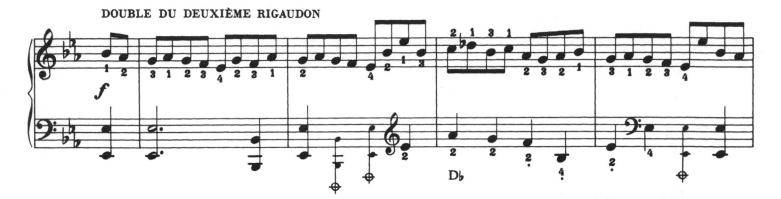

REPRISE DU DOUBLE DU DEUXIÈME RIGAUDON
a tempo

Tambourin

Transcribed for Harp
by Carlos Salzedo
(Revised 1952)

Jean - Philippe Rameau

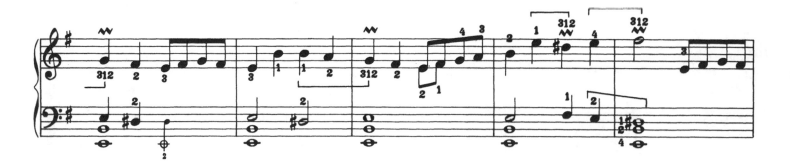

(1) Do not replace the B.

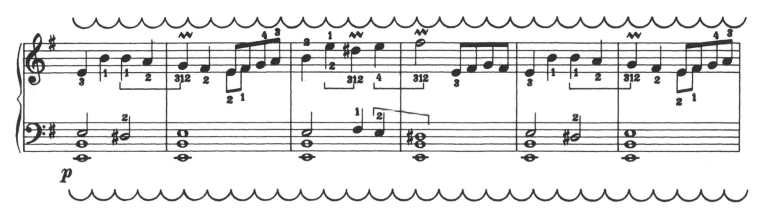

* In this piece, harmonics are written where they actually sound; they are made on the string an octave lower.

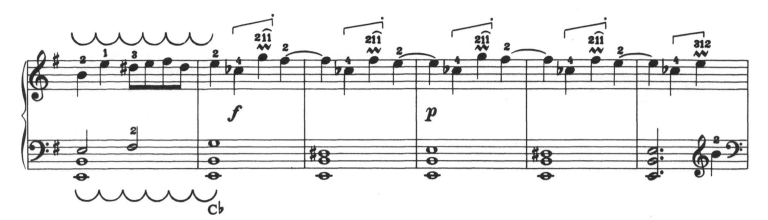

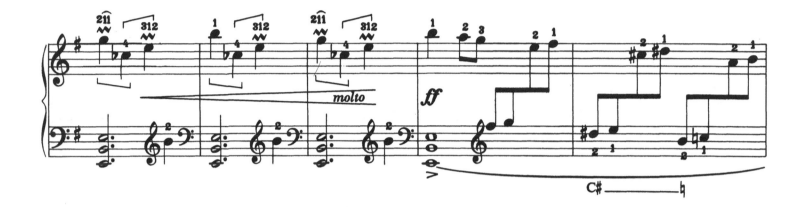

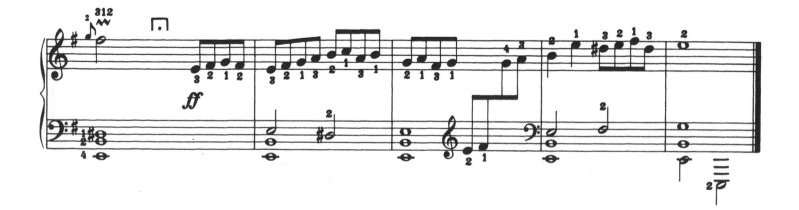

Siciliano

from: Sonata in E♭
for Flute and Cembalo

Transcribed for Harp
by Dewey Owens

Johann Sebastian Bach
(1685 ~ 1750)

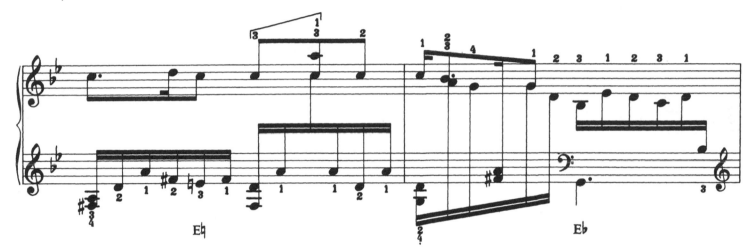

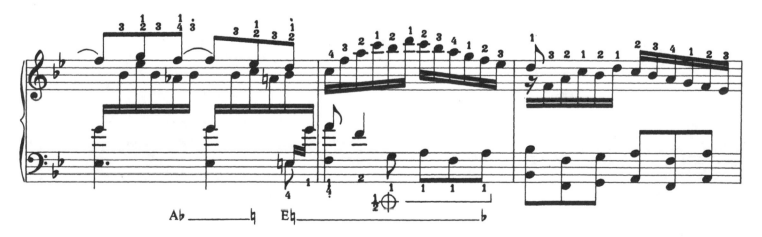

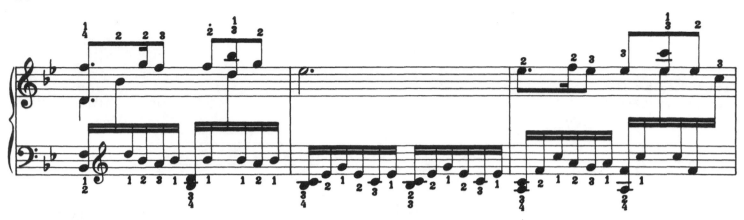

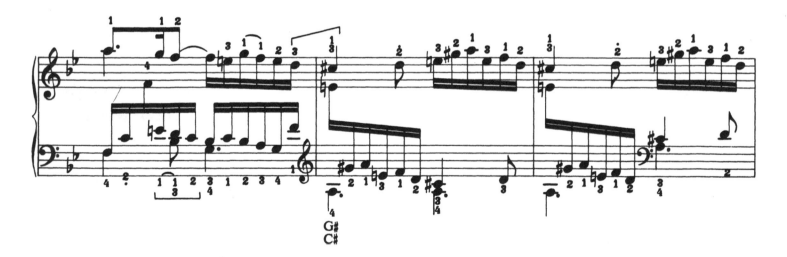

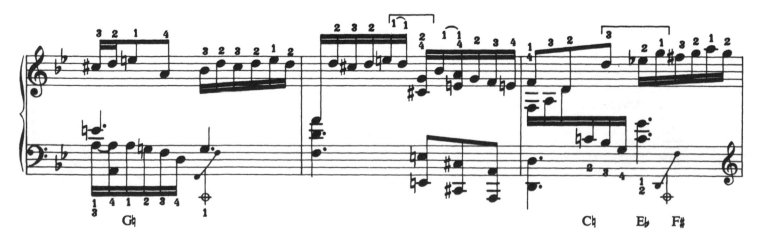

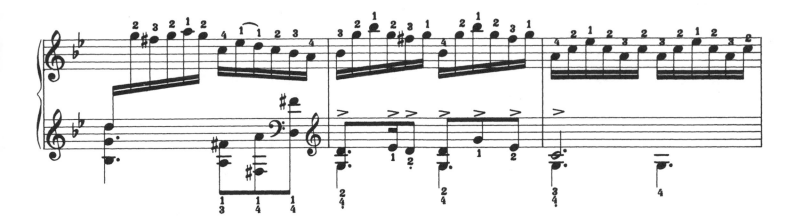

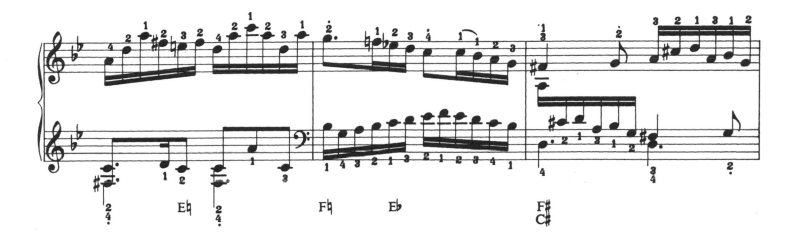

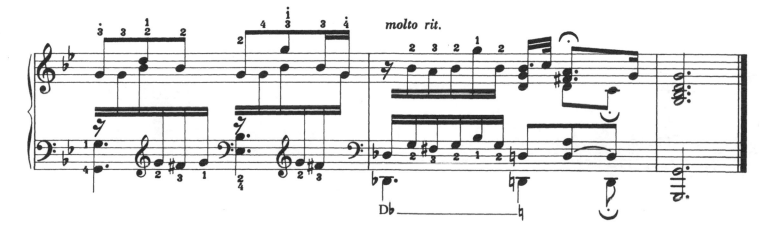

Chaconne

Transcribed for Harp
by Carlos Salzedo

Marie - Auguste Durand
(1830 - 1909)

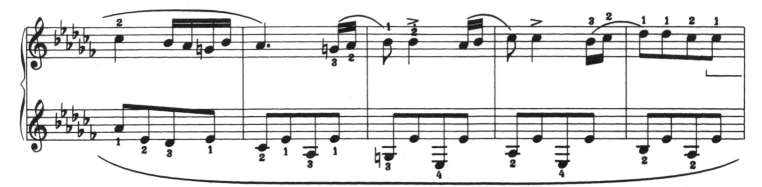

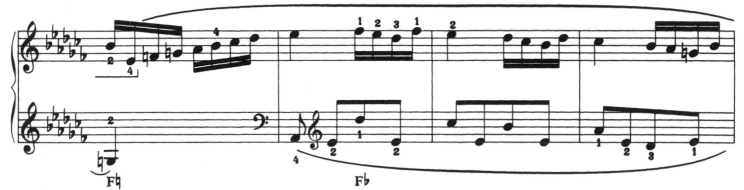

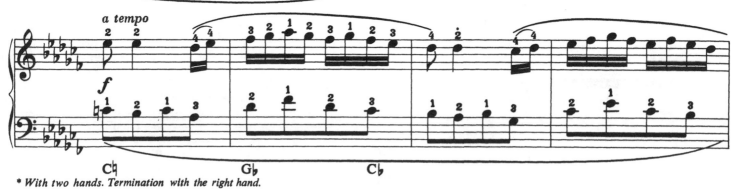

* With two hands. Termination with the right hand.

© *MCMXXIII, by G. Schirmer, Inc.*

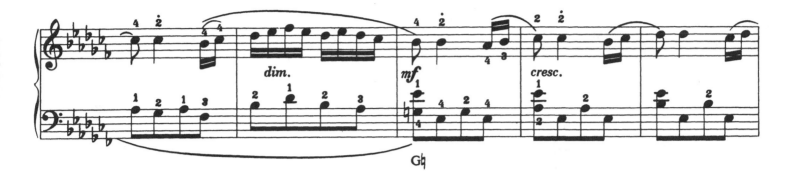

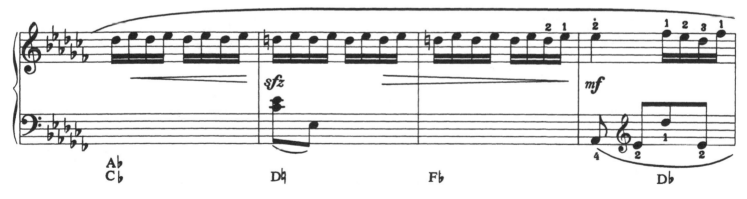

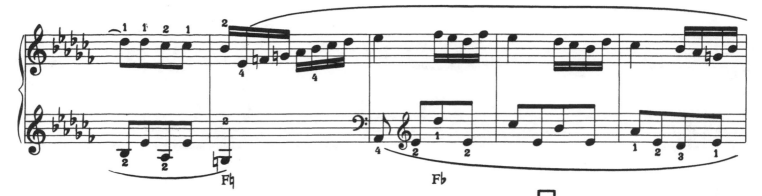

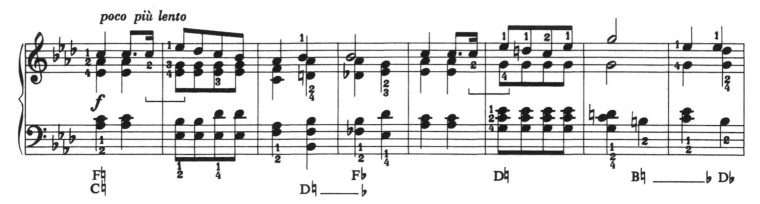

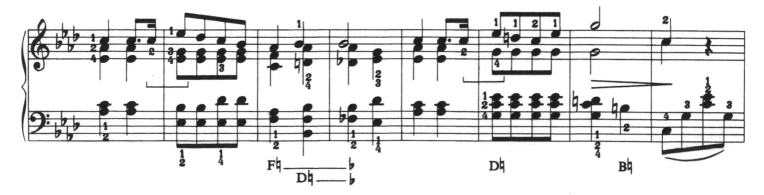

*In this piece, harmonics are written where they actually sound; they are made on the string an octave lower.

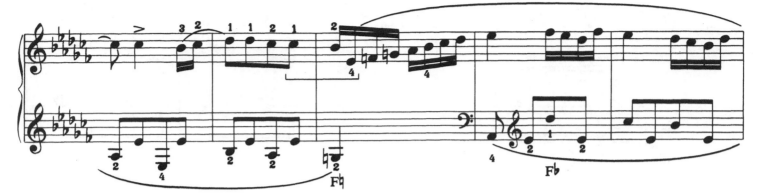

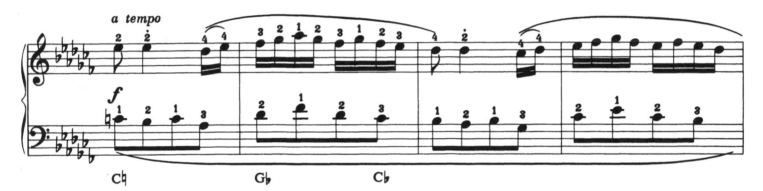

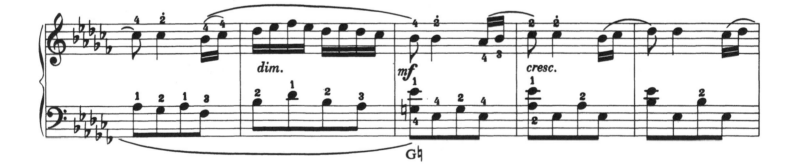

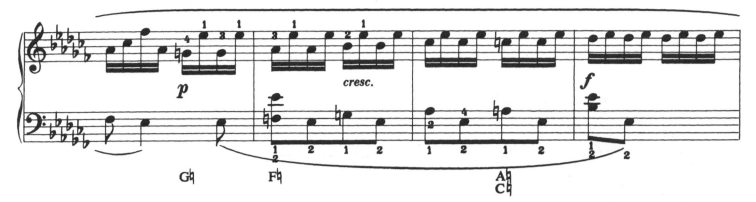

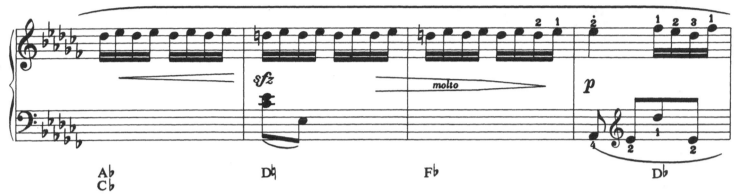

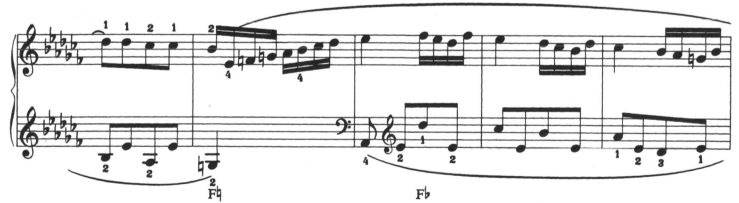

First Arabesque

Transcribed for Harp
by Carlos Salzedo

Claude Debussy
(1862 - 1918)

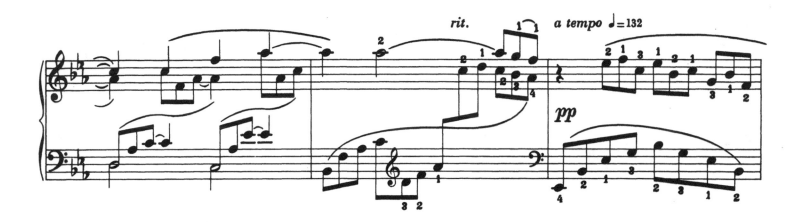

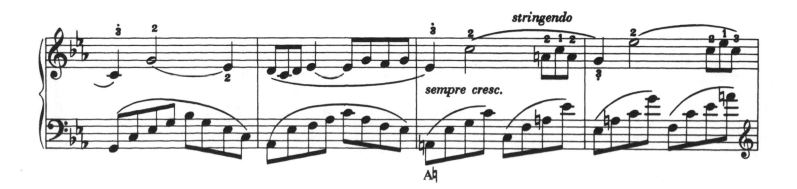

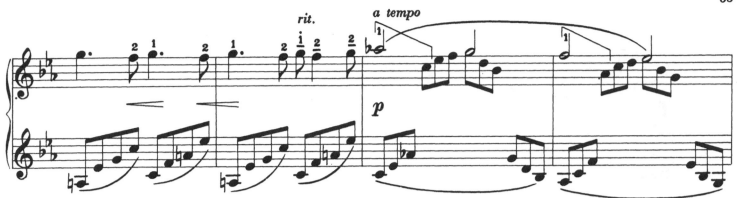

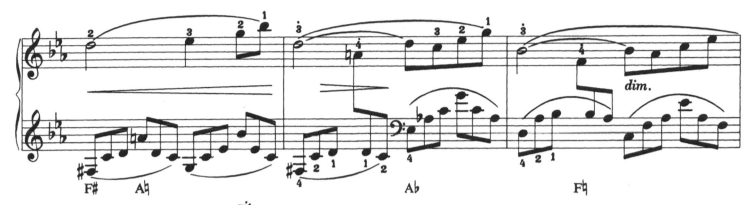

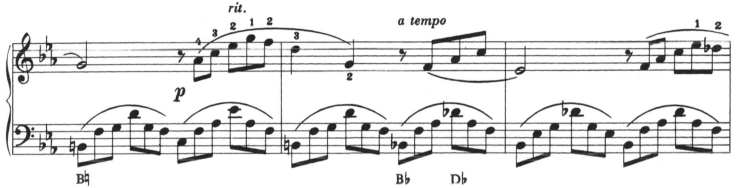

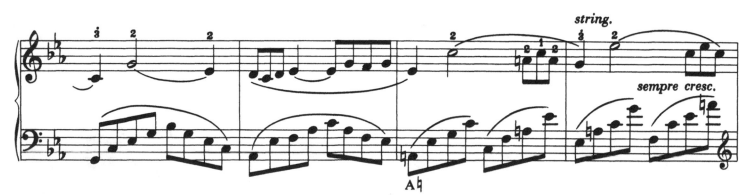

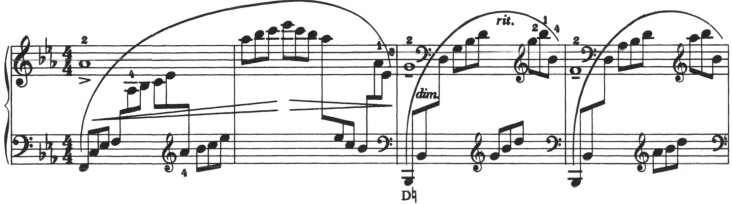

Zarabanda

from: Partita in C

Transcribed for Harp by
Stephanie Rappa-Curcio

Joaquin Turina
(1882 - 1949)

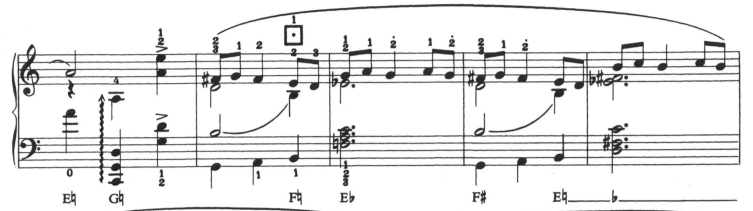

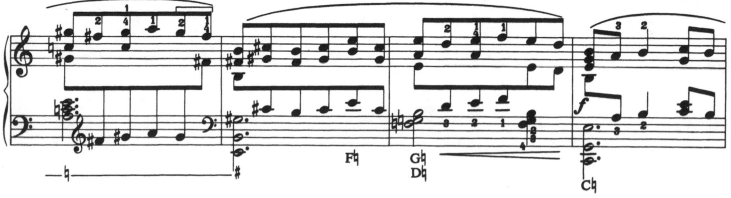

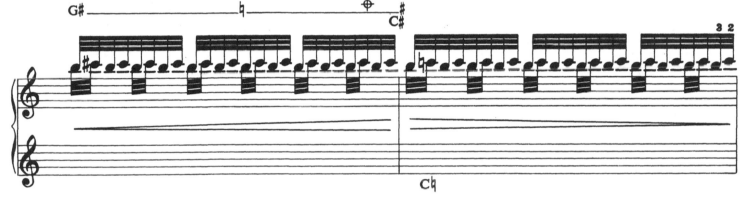

Two Chinese Folk Songs

I

Chou Wen - Chung
(1923 -)

II

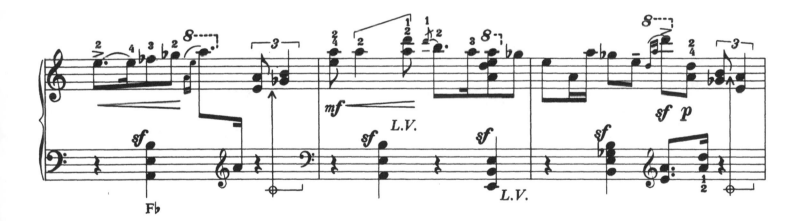

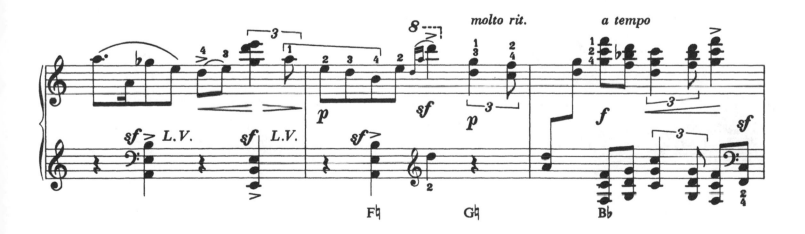

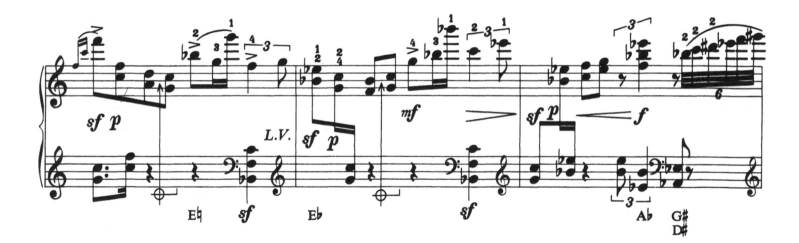

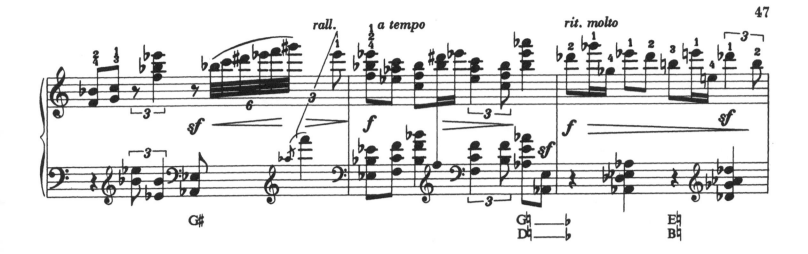

Berceuse

Nicolas Flagello

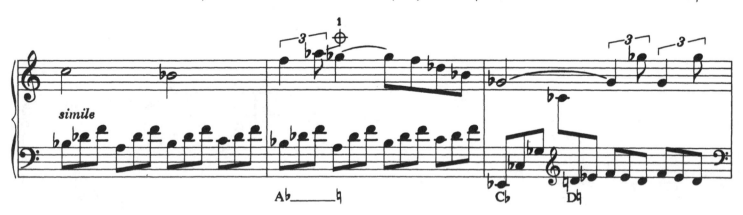

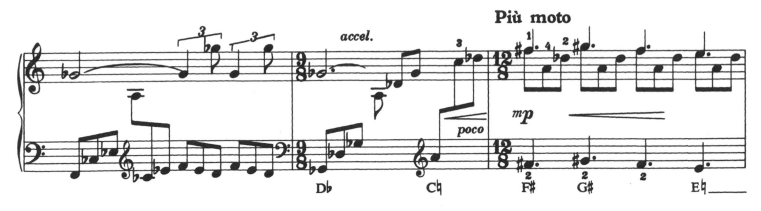

Più agitato

50

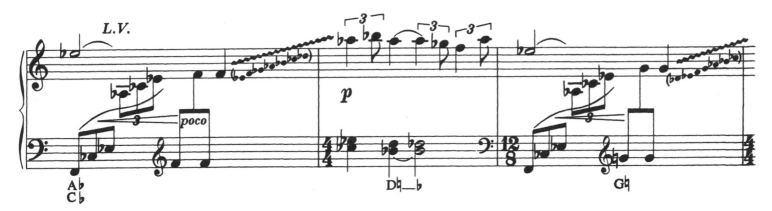

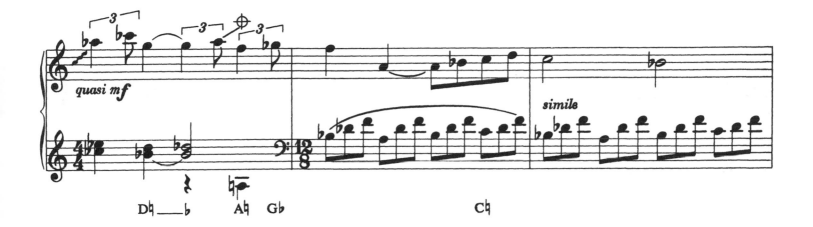

Looking Glass River

Rudolf Forst

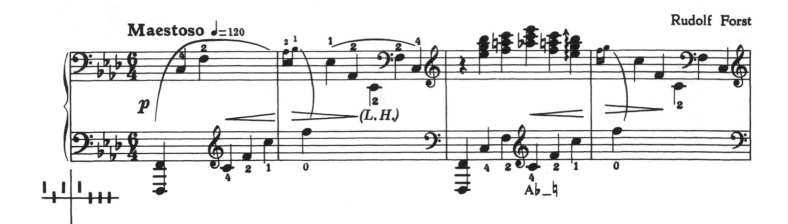

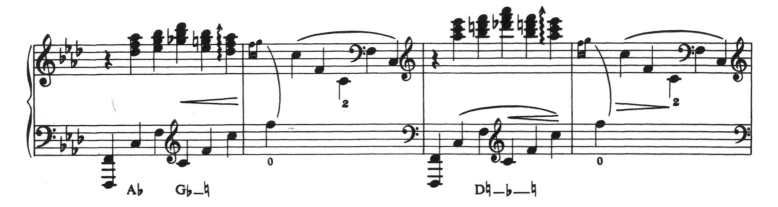

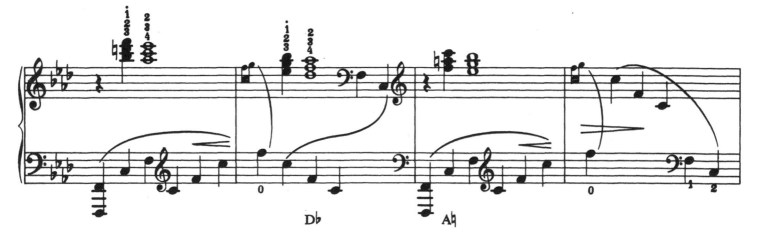

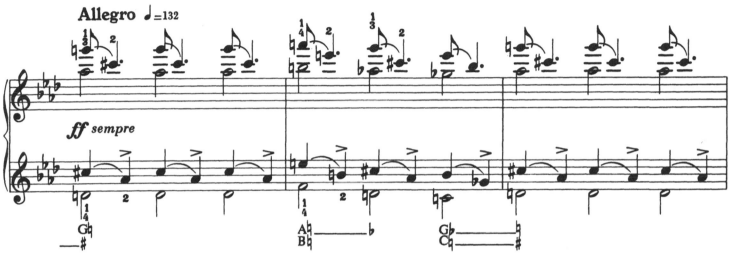

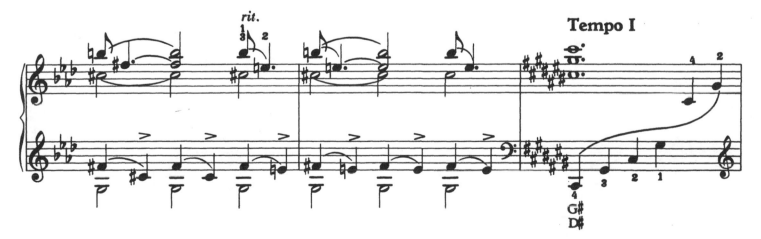

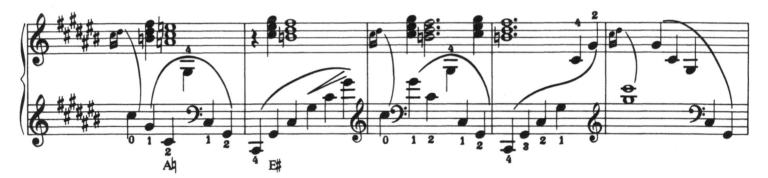

Five Preludes

I

Alojz Srebotnjak

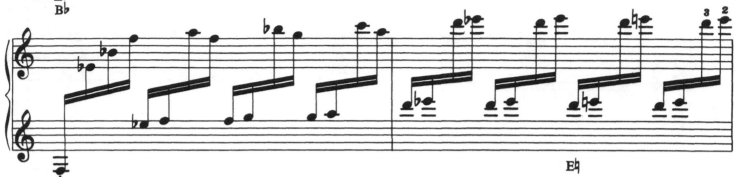

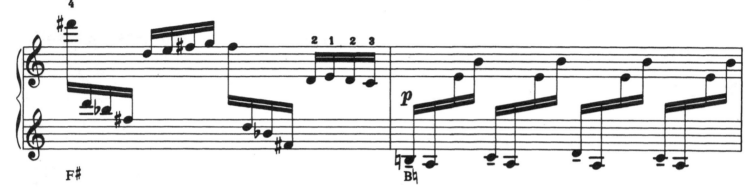

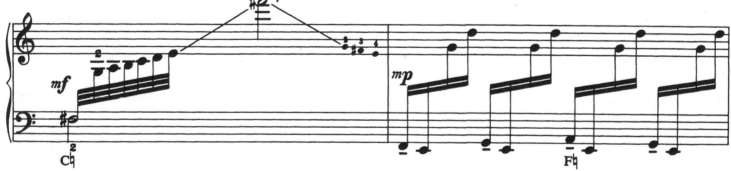

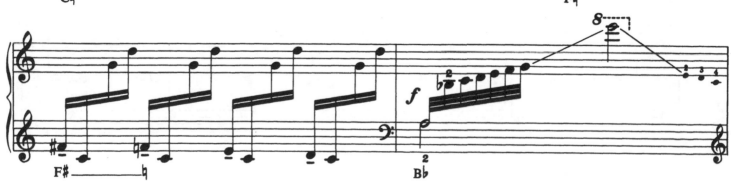

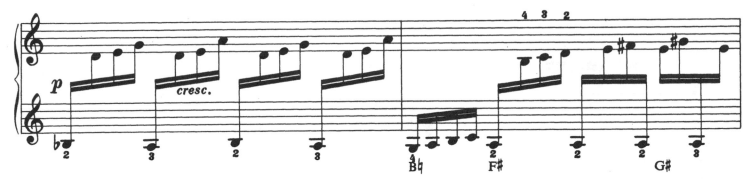

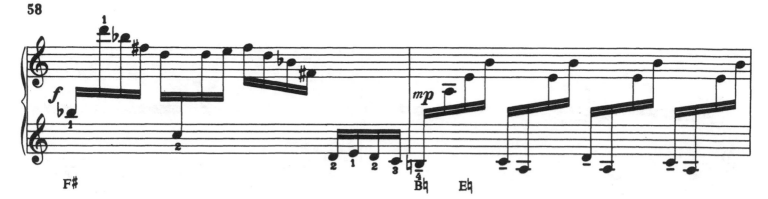

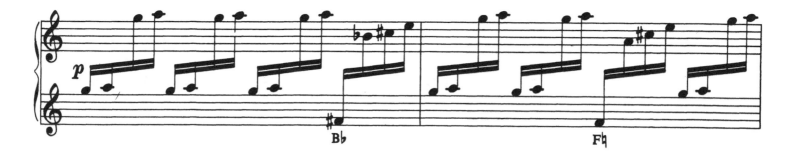

2

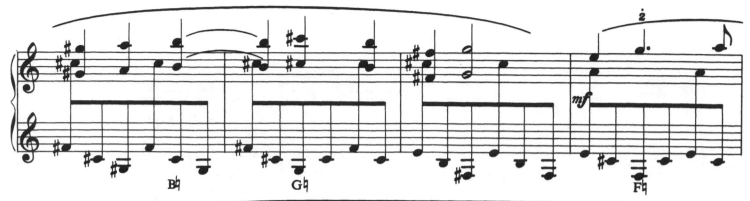

tornando al · Tempo primo

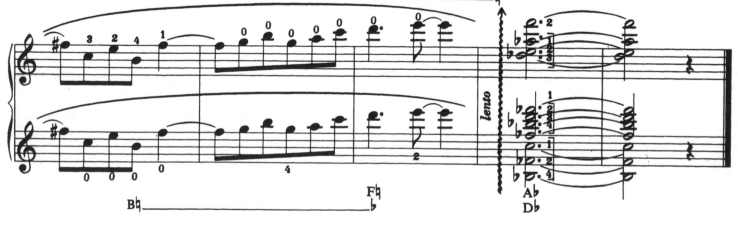

3

Allegretto, leggiero ♩ = 200

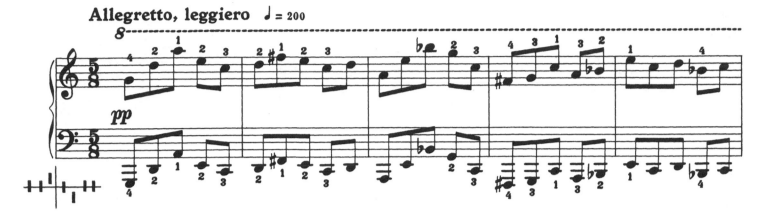

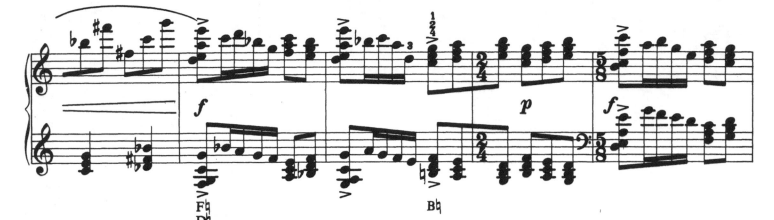

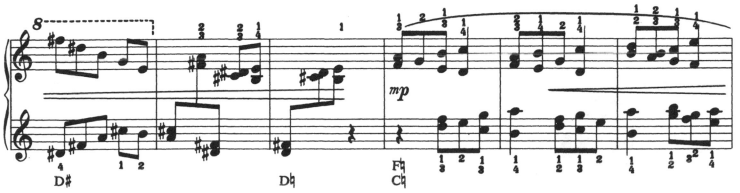

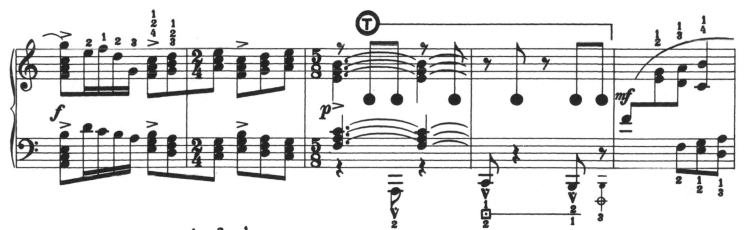

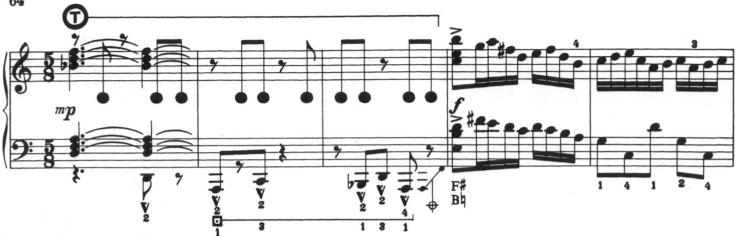

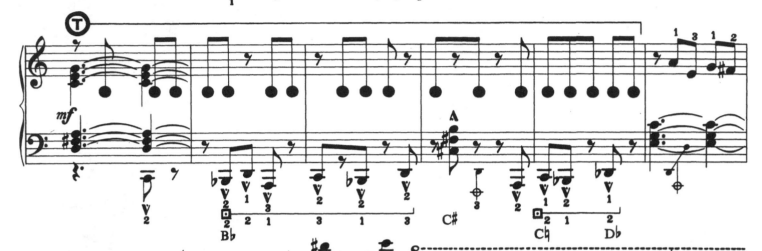

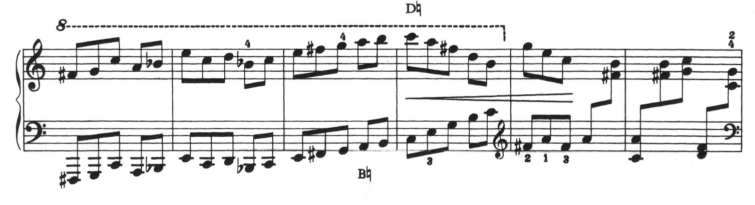

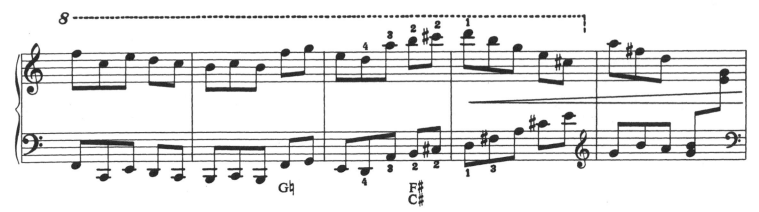

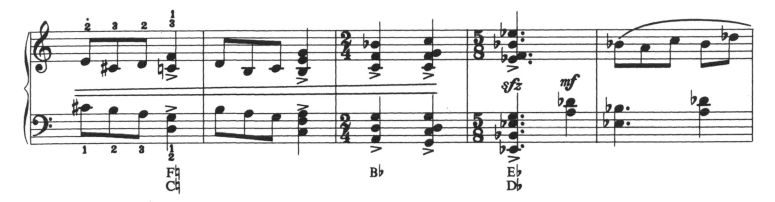

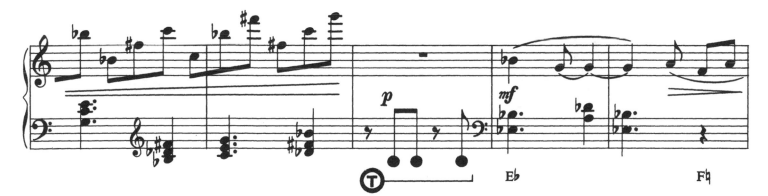

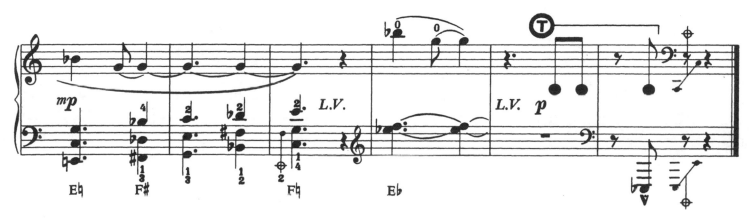

4

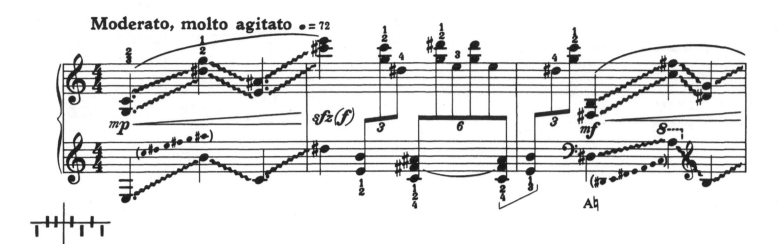

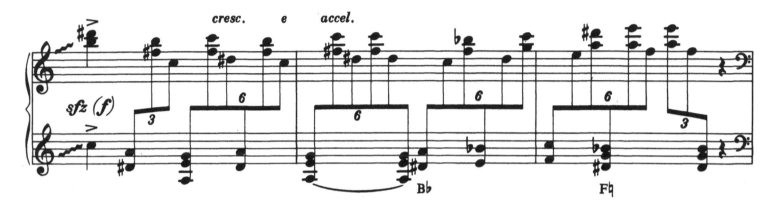

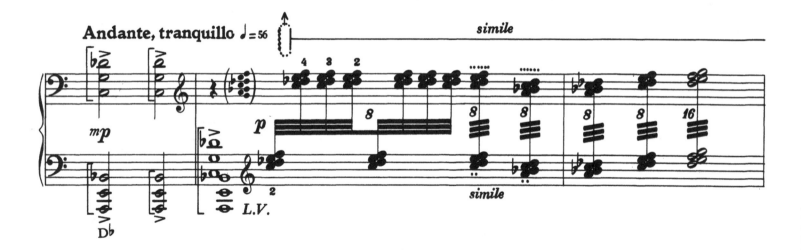

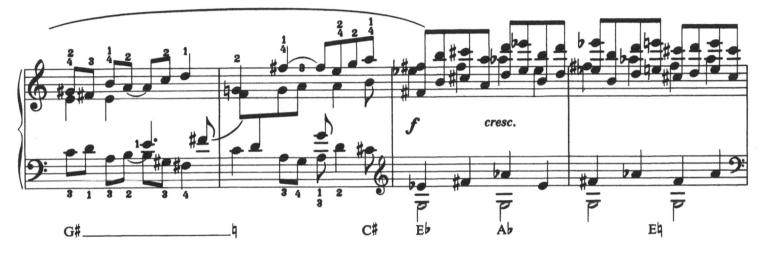

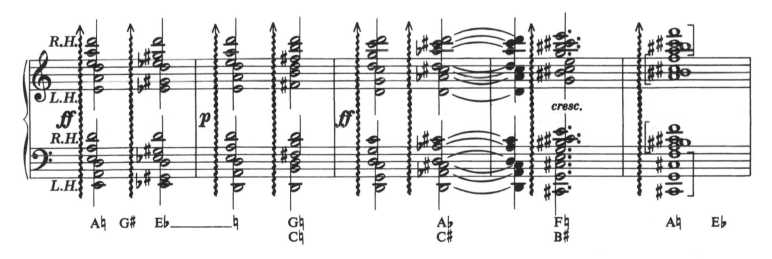

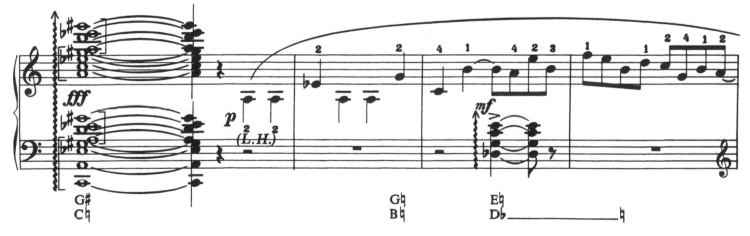

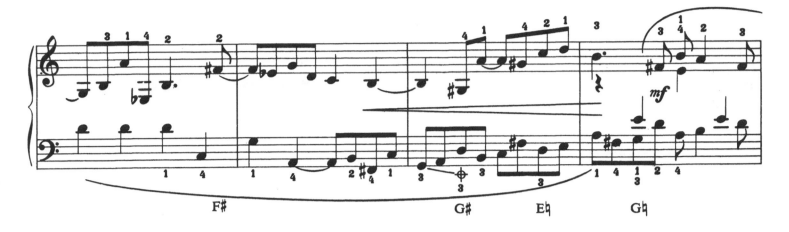

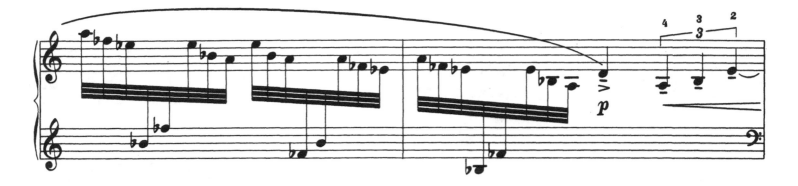

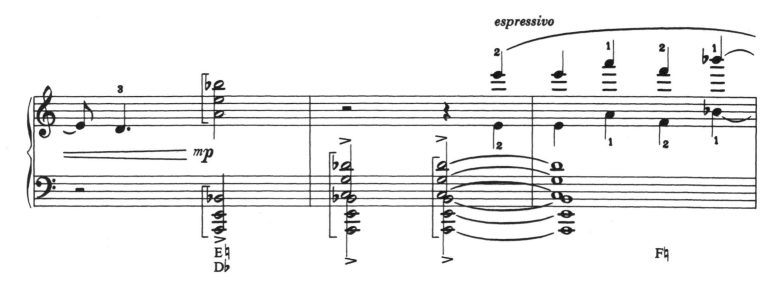

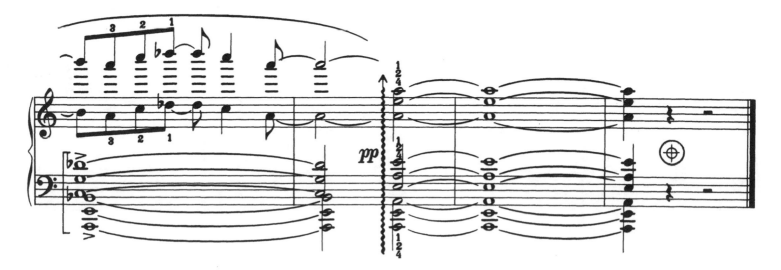

5

Allegro quasi rustico ♩ = 96

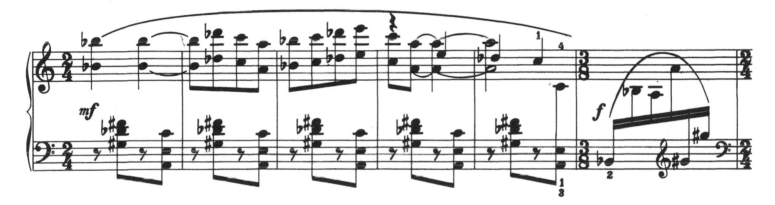

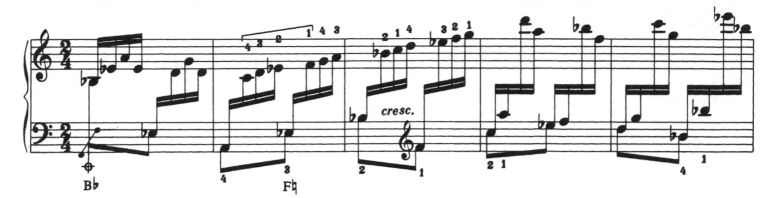

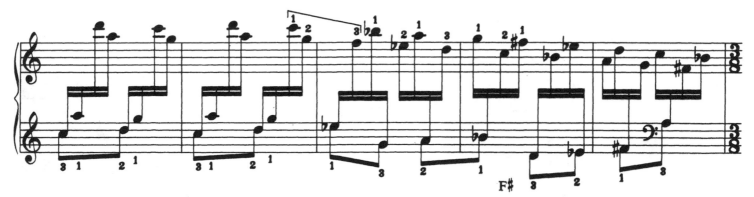

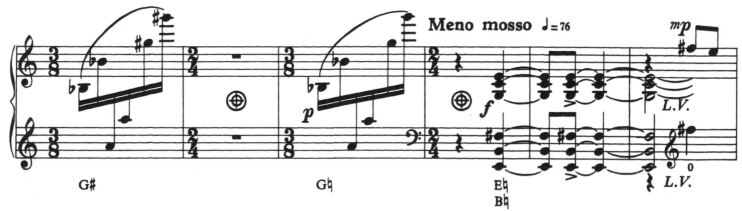

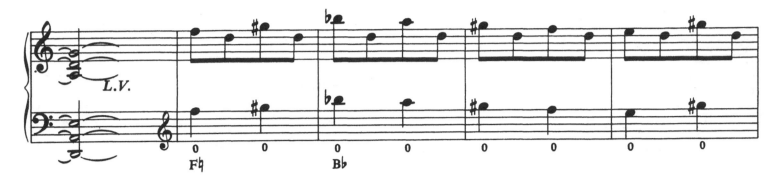

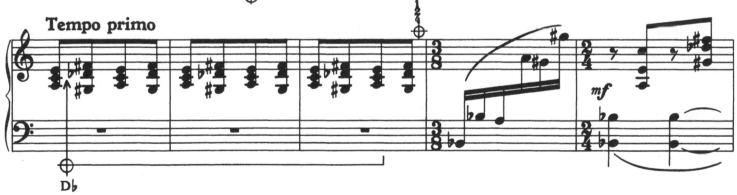

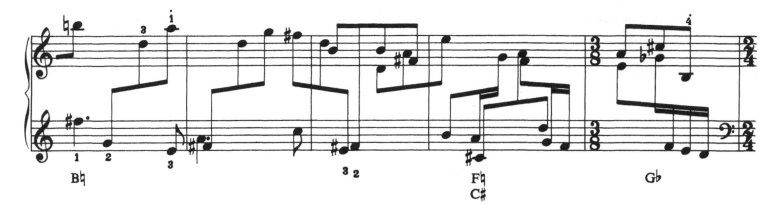

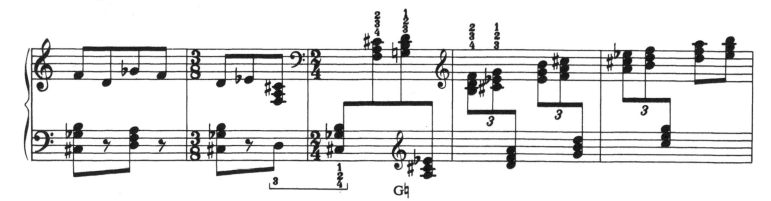